MW01595365

IF YOU FIGHT
YOU WILL WIN

What a Delight to meet you... God's special warrior.
Don't Stop Prayeng !

C Adams 7/18/20

IF YOU FIGHT YOU WILL WIN

The Daily Fighting Manual

Church prayer training series

A Guide To Spiritual Warfare

CELESTINE ODOMS

To order additional copies of this book, contact:
Xlibris Corporation
1-888-795-4274
www.Xlibris.com
Orders@Xlibris.com
74979

CONTENTS

To Jeremiah,
You always remind me of the Power of Prayer,
in practice and in results.

Scriptural references are printed after each chapter.
Unless otherwise noted, all scripture references are
from the King James Version of the Bible.

Father,
I acknowledge your presence
and I ask that you glorify yourself in
these writings. Let this word bless
your people one thousand fold and let all who take
up these pages be anointed with your spirit of
Wisdom, Revelation and Knowledge.
In Jesus Name.

INTRODUCTION

Spiritual warfare is a dynamic force of knowledge that is moving across the Body of Christ today. Christians are becoming more and more aware of the need for it. But what is Spiritual Warfare? How is it different from the praying we are already doing? How do we access it? "IF YOU FIGHT YOU WIN" The Daily Fighting Manual is a practical guide that will help you understand how to do Spiritual Warfare beginning with yourself. "IF YOU FIGHT YOU WIN" is Spiritual Warfare "boot camp". It will give you basic training in how to wage war against the "enemies" of your life. "IF YOU FIGHT YOU WIN", will prepare you for war by giving you daily exercises to increase your awareness of GOD and it will put you to work against the forces of darkness.

Soldiers in any army must be strong, courageous, brave and fortified. Soldiers do not go into battle untrained, unprepared or unequipped. "IF YOU FIGHT YOU WILL WIN" will show you how to personally prepare for warfare by getting you cleansed, purged and pure before GOD. It is designed to help you prepare yourself with a fighting mentality.

As I have ministered in the Body of Christ, I have found that many of us are "Word-fat babies"—and spoiled! We are overfed on the Word of GOD without the demonstration of the Power of GOD. When the enemy comes along with infirmity, discouragement and depression—not to mention the robbing of our finances and the destruction of our families, we sit idly by watching and crying and not using the power we have been given through the Blood of the Lamb. We have the Word, but we have failed to put it into practice. We have failed to use it appropriately to effect sustaining changes for good in our lives. I truly believe that many Christians believe, even if subconsciously, that GOD is blessing them solely so they can "keep up with the Jones" or so they can look down on those who have less. There are social concerns that are a disgrace to humanity—aids, drugs, crime, murder, abortion, pornography, witchcraft and satanism to mention a few. GOD has given us dominion over all of these things, but the Body of Christ is the "Great Sleeping Giant". We have the Blood— we have the Word and all power and authority have been given to us in Jesus' Name but we are not using them to the fullness of their power to rid society of its ills.

"IF YOU FIGHT YOU WIN" is designed to wake you up to who you are in GOD and Who He is to you. This spiritual warfare manual will get you geared up for taking dominion over all the things that GOD had already given you and will put you in contact with Him on a daily basis. We are called to be champions, victorious, triumphant and without defeat in every area of our lives—but we have got to fight! We cannot be victorious and we cannot be champions unless we fight!

Celestine Odoms

IF YOU FIGHT YOU WILL WIN
The Daily Fighting Manual
is based on the
Book of Joshua,
Chapters 1-12.

To prepare for the revelation contained herein,
read these passages in various translations of the Bible.

Chapter 1

WE CAN'T BE CHAMPIONS UNLESS WE FIGHT

Put on the whole armor of GOD, that ye may
be able to stand against the wiles of the devil.
For we wrestle not against flesh and blood,
but against the rulers of the darkness of this world,
against spiritual wickedness in high places.
Wherefore take unto you the whole armor of GOD,
that ye may be able to withstand in the evil day,
and having done all to stand, Stand therefore,
having your loins girt about with truth, having
on the breastplate of righteousness and your feet shod
with the preparation of the gospel of peace;
above all, taking the shield of faith, wherewith ye
shall be able to quench all the fiery darts of the wicked.
And take the helmet of salvation, and the sword of the spirit,
which is the Word of GOD: praying always with all supplication
in the Spirit, and watching thereunto with all perseverance
and supplication for all saints; and for me, that utterance
may be given unto me, that I may open my mouth boldly,
to make known the mystery of the Gospel.
EPHESIANS 6:11 19

Today, the enemy is not playing. He means to rip your head off!! GOD is not playing either. He has equipped us for battle with a formidable foe and unlike Saul's oversized armor on David, our armor is perfectly suited to what we have to do to tear satan's kingdom down. We must take every weapon and every tool that GOD has given us and we must skillfully put them to use against the enemy. As we take on the whole armor of GOD, all weapons and all tools GOD has given us; we need to fully understand that "putting on the whole armor of GOD" is not just a figure of speech. We must be fully trained to use our armor to take the Kingdom back by force, to sustain our place and hold our victories. (Ex.15:3, Ps.18:34)

There is much said about this dispensation being the Joshua Generation—The generation of fighters who are not afraid to take back their belongings by strength and force. We know the promises of GOD and we have crossed over into the Promised Land. We have followed the anointed leaders that GOD has appointed to bring us out by teaching us faith. Now, that we are out of Egypt, now that we have crossed over Jordan . . . we must now—just as Joshua did, fight for every piece of land GOD said is ours. To possess the Land, we must fight and conquer our enemies and drive them out one-by-one not allowing them to return. (Jos.3:9, 10). GOD told us that everywhere the sole of our feet treads is ours (Jos.1:3) and with GOD's instructions, just as Joshua did, we must take back what is ours. That comes through fearless fighters knowing while going into battle that "they that be with us are more than they that be with them"; (IIKings6:16). We must also know that we will conquer our enemies and make an open show of them (Col. 2:15). This DAILY FIGHTING MANUAL is designed to help you develop your personal fighting plan. It will help you strategize against satan and pull down every attack against you, your home, family, church and the Kingdom of GOD.

THE WEAPONS OF OUR WARFARE ARE NOT CARNAL, BUT MIGHTY THROUGH GOD TO THE PULLING DOWN OF STRONGHOLDS. (II CORINTHIANS.10:4)

Our weapons are not the ordinary fleshly tools that the world uses, but GOD has given us extraordinary weaponry in the spirit realm designed to inform us, train us and fortify us (Jer.50:25). We must remember that our battle is not against flesh and blood (Eph.6:12), so the ordinary tactics one would employ in the natural realm will not give a sustaining victory. GOD has called us to triumph (IICor.2:14) to overcome and sustain victory in our battle against principalities, against powers, against the rulers of the darkness of this world, against spiritual wickedness in high places. GOD has given us the weapons necessary to fight them—to take back what they have taken from us and to keep it!—To keep the territory we have gained. But we will not use sticks or stones, or guns in our fight. We will use and employ weapons that are meet to do the job where the battle really is—IN THE SPIRIT REALM!

The weapons that GOD has given us include:

1. Prayer & meditation
2. Canceling the enemy's power in your life
3. Taking on a fighting attitude
4. Confession
5. Drawing positive qualities
6. Giving thanks
7. Judging yourself
8. Taking inventory
9. Forgiveness
10. Coming clean
11. Communion
12. Calling forth your gifts
13. Testimony

IF YOU FIGHT YOU WILL WIN will help you to understand:

- What your requirements are for the battle and will help you to fight and take back what is rightfully yours

- How to prepare strategies for war that will drive the enemy out and not allow him to return
- How to prepare a winning mentality
- How to go to war with confidence for winning

Remember that as you begin to fight, the enemy will retaliate. Be prepared for the counterattacks by asking GOD for wisdom on how to discern and handle the enemy's retaliation.

Victory is yours.

Go into battle knowing that GOD has given all of your enemies to you. Know this before the battle begins . . . while you are in the battle . . . and when the battle is over; you will openly display and expose the enemy. Rejoice going into the battle. Rejoice during the battle and rejoice when the battle is over because—*WE WIN! But we can't be champions unless we fight!*

SCRIPTURAL REFERENCES FOR

CHAPTER 1

WE CAN'T BE CHAMPIONS UNLESS WE FIGHT

Ephesians 6:11-19

Put on the whole armor of GOD that ye may be able to stand against the wiles of the devil. For we wrestle not against flesh and blood, but against the rulers of the darkness of this world, against spiritual wickedness in high places. Wherefore take unto you the whole armor of GOD, that ye may be able to withstand in the evil day, and having done all to stand, Stand therefore, having your loins girt about with truth, having on the breastplate of righteousness and your feet shod with the preparation of the gospel of peace; above all, taking the shield of faith, wherewith ye shall be able to quench all the fiery darts of the wicked. And take the helmet of salvation, and the sword of the spirit, which is the Word of GOD: praying always with all supplication in the Spirit, and watching thereunto with all perseverance and supplication for all saints; and for me, that utterance may be given unto me, that I may open my mouth boldly, to make known the mystery of the Gospel.

Colossians 2:15

And having spoiled principalities and powers, he made a show of them openly, triumphing over them in it.

II Corinthians 10:4

For the weapons of our warfare are not carnal, but mighty through GOD to the pulling down of strongholds.

II Kings 6:16

And he answered, fear not: for they that be with us are more than they that be with them.

Exodus 15:3

The LORD is a man of war: The LORD is his name.

Jeremiah 50:25

The Lord hath opened his armory, and hath brought the weapons of his indignation: for this is the work of the LORD GOD of hosts in the land of the Chaldeans.

II Corinthians 2:14

Now thanks be to GOD, which always causes us to triumph in Christ, and makes manifest the savor of his knowledge by us in every place.

Psalms 18:34

He teaches my hands to war, so that a bow of steel is broken in mine arms.

Joshua 1:3

Every place that the sole of your foot shall tread upon, that have I given unto you, as I said unto Moses.

Study Questions

Chapter 1

CAN'T BE CHAMPIONS UNLESS WE FIGHT

1. What does "Putting on the whole armor of GOD" mean to you?
   _____
   _____
   _____

2. Have you made it a practice to put on the armor of GOD?
   _____
   _____
   _____

3. What armor have you put on in the past and how has it helped you?
   _____
   _____
   _____

4. Are there areas in your life where you could fight for your natural or your spiritual rights?
   _____
   _____
   _____

Chapter 2

KEEP STRONG
FOR THE BATTLE

Be strong in the Lord
And in the power of his might.
Ephesians 6:12 (6:10)

Be strong and of good courage:
Be not afraid, neither be thou dismayed;
For the Lord thy God is with thee,
Whithersoever thou goes.
Joshua 1:4 (1:9)

To keep strong for the battle that GOD has set before you—to take the kingdom by force—we must be alert and aware (Eph. 5:14).

We must take on an attitude for fighting each day. The enemy is not taking any breaks from the fight he is waging against you and you must not take any breaks either. In fact, you must be more alert than ever to stay ahead of the enemy's devices. GOD has made promises to us in His Word through His Son, Jesus. You've got to keep abreast of your rights in Jesus. If you are ignorant of your rights, satan will keep them from you.

Knowing the Covenant promises of GOD is basic Christianity.

Walking in GOD's Covenant is essential to who we are in Christ. Unfortunately, the Church has focused its primary attention on many things that are secondary to teaching people what GOD has granted them as believers in Christ. There are actual benefits to receiving Jesus as Savior. Most people are so glad just to be saved, because they are usually saved from something like drugs, adultery, life of crime, gangs, etc. They are very thankful and rightly so. But they must be grounded in the Covenant GOD has given along with receiving Jesus.

The Covenant promises of GOD should be "Christianity 101". They should be taught and re-taught and reviewed regularly as new Christians are being saved and added to the church each day. We see too many Christians who have been Born Again for 10—15—25 years and haven't known one full week of peace—who do not know how to flow in Joy, who are still fighting infirmity and poverty.

The Covenant Promises of GOD must be anchored in our spirits. We must walk them and talk them. We must know them inside and out and be able to use them in warfare against the enemy who wants to and usually succeeds in stealing them away from us. We must anchor them in our spirits so that nothing can remove them. So that nothing can separate us from them.

Keeping strong for the battle means:

- Knowing GOD's promises to you
- Knowing GOD has established a Covenant with you through Jesus
- You must know GOD's Covenant promises to you and remind yourself and satan of them daily. The Covenant promises are:

Perfect Peace (John16:33)
Everlasting Life (John3:16)
Abundant Life (John 10:10)
Fullness of Joy (John15:11)

Divine Health (III John 2)
Deliverance (Luke 4:16)
Prosperity (IIIJohn2)

MEDITATE ON THE PROMISES OF GOD

If you are not walking in the fullness of GOD's Covenant with us, then you must learn how to prepare strategies to go into the enemy's camp and take your blessings back. GOD has already provided you with His Covenant Blessings; if you are not realizing them, it's because the prince of this world is holding them up. So, go and get them back! Your enemy doesn't want you strong and fortified in peace, joy, abundant life, health, prosperity and deliverance. When you have all these blessings going for you, you are walking in victory and spoiling his plans for you.

When you walk in victory, satan can't mess with you. Begin to fortify your boundaries and build walls of strength around your mind, around your body and around your spirit with peace (satan hates peace!). Enter into Jesus' Peace and allow it to flood your heart and mind.

Fortify yourself with joy.

Always keep and maintain your Joy. Always be full of GOD's Joy. Laugh at the devil when he tries to steal, kill or destroy something in your life. Psalm 1 says that GOD puts our enemy into derision. GOD laughs at the devil! You may as well do the same. The devil hates laughter and your laughter will confuse him and his plans for your destruction.

THE JOY OF THE LORD IS YOUR STRENGTH.
GOD MOVES THROUGH PEACE AND JOY

The Peace of Jesus, which surpasses all understanding, and the Joy of the LORD are foundations for all other blessings.

GOD always moves in a blanket of Peace.

Wherever His presence is there is Peace and He comes to make us glad and not sad. Unfortunately, your enemy is aware of this and will always send attacks against your peace and your joy. When he does this, he is attacking the very foundation of your strength in GOD. If he can get you outside of your covenant of peace and joy, then he can cause other catastrophes in your life. He works through you when you are upset and imbalanced in your mind. How can you have mental balance when you are upset, frustrated, worried, depressed and distraught? When the enemy begins to attack you and retaliate against you because of your warfare against him, you must not allow him to anchor his attacks of confusion, turmoil, chaos, vexation, heaviness, discouragement and depression in you.

YOU MUST FIGHT TO KEEP YOUR BLESSINGS OF PEACE AND JOY!

Fight him with what GOD has said in His Word. Tell the devil that your peace *is* perfect (Isa.26:3) and your Joy is full (John15:11) and to "GET THEE HENCE!". If you have to tell him 100 times a day, do it! Your enemy will do all that he knows to steal your focus off GOD's promises, so be alert and aware of his tactics. The devil's plan is to continue his siege until the peace that Jesus gave you is broken to the degree that you cannot retrieve it and until your joy—the very joy of the LORD Himself — is gone. I am so protective of my peace and my joy and I know that if I allow him to take them, I am a goner.

We must know that, no matter what the enemy sends our way, WE MUST MAINTAIN JOY AT ALL COST! WE MUST MAINTAIN PEACE AT ALL COST!

Since you already know that the enemy's tactics are to steal your joy and your peace, be prepared for him. Make up your mind that you will not allow him to do that and fight him with the Word of GOD. **FIGHT HIM WITH EVERY WEAPON**

YOU HAVE HEAD-TO-HEAD AND TOE-TO-TOE UNTIL HE LEAVES.

PREPARE YOURSELF

Prepare yourself daily in prayer, reading the Word (II Tim. 2:15) and surrendering to GOD everything in you that is not like Him. **We must keep correct associations,** remembering to associate with those who are going in the same direction as we are, those who stir us up spiritually (II Cor.6:17) Incorrect associations can be implants by the enemy to keep you in turmoil. If your associations stir you up in gossip, backbiting, church hopping then LET THEM GO! **Your battle should begin the minute you awake and your pace for the day should be set in the first fifteen minutes of the day.** Smith Wigglesworth, a great man of GOD, responsible for bringing over 40 people back from the dead and many other miraculous healings, did not get out of bed until he had Communion with the LORD. What a way to start the day!

The enemy does not hang around in a Word environment.

As you study the Word of GOD, it can be available to you many genres. Today the Word of GOD is not just written, you can get the Bible on CD's, DVD's, and acted out in videos and movies. Keep a set of the scriptures in your house and another for your car. Listening to the scriptures when you cannot read them will help you in your daily fortification.

TO KEEP STRONG DO THIS DAILY

1. Set your pace for the day in the first fifteen minutes you awake.
2. Study the Word of GOD
3. Pray fervently
4. Meditate on GOD's Covenant with you for:

       PEACE
       JOY

ABUNDANT LIFE
HEALTH
PROSPERITY
DELIVERANCE

5. Take on a fighting attitude and keep it.
6. Keep correct associations.
7. Surrender everything in you not like GOD.
8. Partake of the LORD'S SUPPER each day.
9. Prepare strategies to go into the enemy's territory.

SCRIPTURAL REFERENCES FOR

CHAPTER 2

KEEP STRONG FOR THE BATTLE

Joshua 1:9

Be strong and of good courage; be not afraid, neither be thou dismayed for the LORD thy GOD is with thee whithersoever thou goes.

Ephesians 5:14

Wherefore he said, awake thou that sleeps, and arise from the dead and Christ shall give you light.

II Timothy 2:15

Study to show thyself approved unto GOD. a workman that needs not to be ashamed, rightly dividing the WORD of TRUTH.

II Corinthians 6:17

Wherefore come out from among them and be ye separate, says the LORD, and touch not the unclean thing. And I will receive you.

COVENANT SCRIPTURES

Luke 4:18

The Spirit of the LORD is upon me, because He hast anointed me to preach the gospel to the poor; he hath sent me to heal the brokenhearted, and to preach deliverance to the captives, and the recovering of sight to the blind, to set at liberty them that are bruised.

John 3:16

For GOD so loved the world, that He gave His only begotten Son, that whosoever believeth on Him should not perish, but have everlasting life.

John 10:10

The thief cometh not, but for to steal, kill and to destroy: I am come that they might have life and that they might have it more abundantly.

John 6:57

As the living Father hath, sent me, and I live by the Father: so he that eats me, even he shall live by me.

I Peter 2:24

Who his own self bare our sins in his own body on the tree, that we, being dead to sins, should live to righteousness: by whose stripes ye were healed.

III John 2

Beloved I wish above all things that thou may prosper and be in health even as your soul prospers.

John 16:33

These things I have spoken unto you, that in me ye might have peace. In the world, ye shall have tribulation: but be of good cheer, I have overcome the world.

John 15:11

These things have I spoken unto you, that my joy might remain in you and that your joy might be full.

Study Questions

CHAPTER 2

KEEP STRONG FOR THE BATTLE

1. How can you prepare yourself for warfare for the day?

   _____

   _____

   _____

2. What weapons would be most beneficial to you right now?

   _____

   _____

   _____

3. Why are these weapons beneficial?

   _____

   _____

   _____

4. How can studying the Bible help you with your plan?

   _____

   _____

   _____

5. What other ways can you make sure that the Word of GOD is available to you at all times?

   _____

   _____

   _____

6. What does meditate on GOD's Word mean to you?

   _____

   _____

   _____

7. Why is it important to fortify yourself with the Word of GOD?

_____

_____

_____

8. What is the first thing you can do to keep strong for the battle?

_____

_____

_____

9. Why do we need to fight for what GOD said is ours?

_____

_____

_____

10. What can you do to maintain an attitude of joy and peace?

_____

_____

_____

Chapter 3

WHAT GIANTS CAN
I EAT TODAY?
(A Fighting Attitude)

Only rebel not ye against the Lord,
neither fear ye the people of the land:
for they are bread for us:
their defense is departed from them,
and the Lord is with us: fear them not.
Numbers 14:9

You must get the jump on satan! You must get him before he can get to you. You must wake up with an alert fighting mentality. And when you do, GOD will allow you to scope out satan's tactics against you, your family, your church and you will be ahead of him. GOD will actually give you strategies to counteract the strategy being sent against you.

Wake up each day ready for battle. Wake up each day with the attitude, "What giants can I eat today?" "What's out there?" "What missiles does the enemy have aimed at me today?" And when you find out, be prepared to take each "giant" out and shoot each missile down. You can be certain that he has something aimed at you to bring you down, but you have the authority to stop all darts and weapons used against you. "No weapon formed against you shall prosper."(Isa.54:17)

As Joshua approached the Promised Land, Caleb said, "Let us go up at once and possess it for we are well able to overcome it." (Num.13:30) But the ten scouts with the evil report said, "There are giants in the land. We are in our own sight as grasshoppers to them."(Numbers 13:33) But Joshua said, "They are bread to us." (Numbers 14:9) In other words, *"WE EAT GIANTS FOR LUNCH!!"* LET THIS BE YOUR ATTITUDE AS YOU APPROACH THE DAY. "WHAT GIANTS CAN I EAT TODAY? They are bread to me!" As you approach the principalities over your life and all that is keeping you from entering into the Promised Land—as you approach all evil and spiritual wickedness that are keeping you from the promised blessings of the New Covenant of:

- Life, more abundant
- Divine Health, above all things
- Peace, unspeakable and full of glory
- Prosperity, above all things
- Deliverance, for body mind and soul
- Fullness of Joy
- Unconditional Love

PUT A GIANT ON YOUR MENU EVERY DAY AND WATCH HOW GOD WILL CAUSE THEM TO FALL ONE-BY-ONE.

Psalm 18:34, 37 40 says:
He teaches my hands to war so
that a bow of steel is broken by
mine arms. I have pursued mine
enemies, and overtaken them:
neither did I turn again till
they were consumed. I have
wounded them that they were not
able to rise: They are fallen

> *under my feet. For thou hast*
> *girded me with strength unto*
> *the battle: thou hast subdued*
> *under me those that rose up*
> *against me Thou hast given*
> *me the neck of my enemies:*
> *That I might destroy them that*
> *hate me.*

Be more alert and aware of what is going in the spirit realm. Ephesians 5:14-17 *says:* wherefore he says, awake thou that sleeps and arise from the dead, and Christ shall give you light. See then that ye walk circumspectly, not as fools, but as wise, redeeming the time, because the days are evil. Wherefore be ye not unwise, but understanding what the will of the Lord is.

Wake up thou that slumbers and be aware of what is going on around you. Zero in on and scope out the territory. You must know who and what you are dealing with. Be alert to what GOD is showing you about yourself and others around you.

Don't let any awareness slip. Check everything you perceive and see with the Word of GOD. This is the time to pray for a greater discernment of good and evil. Learn to embrace the good and kick the evil out. Also, learn to hear the voice of GOD and do what He says.

Put a giant on your menu every day and "eat 'em up" with the Word of GOD. In the next chapter, you will get an idea of some of the giants that the enemy sends your way. As you daily use this fighting manual, The Holy Spirit will reveal to you more and more what you are fighting against. As you list your enemies, each day you will learn how to make those giants "bread for you".

Do not be afraid or dismayed, BE STRONG AND OF GOOD COURAGE. (Joshua 1:9) for thus shall the LORD do to all your enemies. Because GOD has gotten you the victory (Psalm 98:1), He will cause you to make an open show of all of your enemies (1Cor.15:17) after they have been slain. **Ask the Father to teach you to fight (Ps.18:34 . . . to show you how to be an alert aware fighter—to show you what you are fighting against.** *IF YOU*

FIGHT, YOU WILL WIN. You cannot fight an enemy you do not see and you cannot be a champion—you cannot be victorious unless you fight!!

Cancel the enemy's power in your life

After GOD has revealed the enemy and where he is hiding: CANCEL OUT THE ENEMY'S POWER IN YOUR LIFE! CANCEL THE ENEMY'S POWER IN YOUR LIFE BY SENDING CONFUSION INTO HIS CAMP. I COR 14:33, PS. 34:4, EVERYTHING THAT HE LAUNCHED AGAINST YOU, SEND IT BACK TO HIM. WE MUST KILL THE GIANTS IN OUR LIVES. WE MUST CUT OFF THE HEADS OF THE GIANTS IN OUR LIVES BY HAVING SPIRITUAL RUTHLESSNESS. REMEMBER TO:

- wake up each day ready for battle
- be alert and awake
- keep a fighting attitude
- do not be afraid
- ask the Father to teach you to fight and show you what you are fighting against.
- cancel the enemy's power in your life by sending confusion back into his camp

SCRIPTURAL REFERENCES FOR

CHAPTER 3

WHAT GIANTS CAN I EAT TODAY?

NUMBERS 13:30, 33

And Caleb stilled the people before Moses and said, Let us go up at once, and possess it; for we are well able to overcome it. And there we saw the giants: and we were in our own sight as grasshoppers, and so we were in their sight.

NUMBERS 14:9

Only rebel not ye against the Lord, neither fear ye the people of the land: for they are bread for us: their defense is departed from them, and the Lord is with us: fear them not.

EPHESIANS 5:14-17

Wherefore he says, AWAKE THOU THAT SLEEPEST, AND ARISE FROM THE DEAD AND CHRIST SHALL GIVE THEE LIGHT. See then that ye walk circumspectly, not as fools, but as wise, redeeming the time, because the days are evil. Wherefore be ye not unwise, but understanding what the will of the Lord is.

PSALMS 18:34, 37

He teaches my hands to war, so that a bow of steel is broken in my arms, I have pursued mine enemies, and overtaken them: neither did I turn again till they were consumed.

I CORINTHIANS 15:27

For He hath put all things under his feet, but when he says all things are put under him, it is manifest that he is excepted, which did put all things under him.

I CORINTHIANS 15:57

But thanks be to GOD which gives us the victory through our Lord Jesus Christ.

I CORINTHIANS 14:33

For GOD is not the author of confusion, but of peace, as in all churches of the saints.

PSALMS 98:1

Sing unto the Lord a new song: for He hath done marvelous things: His right hand, and His holy arm, hath gotten Him the victory.

PSALMS 35:4

Let them be confounded and put to shame that seek after my soul: let them be turned back and brought to confusion that desire my hurt.

Study Questions

Chapter 3

WHAT GIANTS CAN I EAT TODAY?

1. What is hindering you?

   _____

   _____

   _____

2. What obstacles have you made giants in your life?

   _____

   _____

   _____

3. What can you begin to do to overcome your giants?

   _____

   _____

   _____

4. How can you be more aware of what is going on inside you?

   _____

   _____

   _____

5. What can you do to be more aware of the attacks the enemy is waging against your thinking?

   _____

   _____

   _____

6. Can you identify any personal enemies you can fight against?

   _____

   _____

   _____

7. How do you really feel about taking on your fight?

   _____

   _____

   _____

8. How do you feel about fighting against the enemies in your life?

   _____

   _____

   _____

9. How can you wake up each day prepared to fight?

   _____

   _____

   _____

10. What does spiritual ruthlessness mean to you?

   _____

   _____

   _____

Chapter 4

FIGHT TO KILL

And the lord, said to Joshua,
Fear them not: for I have
Delivered them into thine hand;
There shall not a man of them
Stand before thee.
(Joshua 10:8)

Your enemy, the devil, is blocking and has control over what GOD said is yours. GOD has already promised us through the Covenant of the Blood of Jesus to write His Words in our hearts. GOD has promised us abundant life, perfect peace, fullness of joy, divine health, deliverance, prosperity and everlasting life. If you are not walking in these promises, it isn't because GOD has not given them. The Word of GOD does not lie. "It is impossible for GOD to lie." (Hebrews 6:18) Why aren't you walking in the fullness of GOD'S Covenant to you? Because the prince of this world, satan, is holding them up! We must take back what is rightfully ours, but the enemy is not going to let go without a fight. So you must fight him. You must go across enemy lines and destroy his strongholds over your life. Don't worry and don't be afraid: "Have I not commanded thee? Only be thou strong and of good courage; be not afraid, neither be thou dismayed: for the LORD thy GOD is with thee withersoever thou goes." (Joshua 1:9)

FIGHT!! SMITE!! SLAY!!

HE TRAINS ME FOR BATTLE SO
I CAN USE THE STRONGEST BOW.
PSALMS 18:34

**We are in a fight and before we can
fight and watch for anyone else,
we must learn to fight for ourselves.**

It is time for you to tell the devil, "OK devil, no more Mr. Nice Guy! I am crossing the line. I am going to get mine. I will sacrifice etiquette and protocol, because you use them against me. No more bowing to your rules."

Principalities, rulers of darkness and spiritual wickedness in high places are holding your weaknesses and your ignorance against you. They are pressing against you — fighting against you every second of the day. Principalities, rulers of darkness and spiritual wickedness in high places over your city, over your state, over your region are all coming against you to keep you from partaking of the new Covenant of peace in Jesus—of life more abundantly.

FIGHT TO KILL ALL OF YOUR ENEMIES.
DO NOT FEAR THE ENEMY.
FOR GOD HAS DELIVERED THEM INTO YOUR HAND
AND NOT ONE SHALL STAND BEFORE YOU. (JOSHUA 10:8)

SPIRITUAL RUTHLESSNESS

Learn to operate in spiritual ruthlessness, pertaining to obeying GOD at all cost. Do not have any pity for satan, and do not give him any mercy (Psalm 18:41). Tear down his kingdom whenever found by using all the weapons GOD has given you.

The Covenant Promises of GOD are weapons against satan's kingdom. Meditate on them daily (I Tim. 4:15). And speak them out of your mouth against the forces of darkness that don't want you to have them. (Joshua 1:8)

PURSUE YOUR ENEMY!!

Christians have been on the defensive to long running from the devil. It is time for you to run your enemy down and kill him! And do not allow him to return to where you cast him out of. (Joshua 10:19; Psalms 18:37) Utterly destroy all of your enemies! (Joshua 10:36; Psalms 18:40) Leave none remaining! (Joshua 10:33, Psalm 18:39)

Destroy all that breathes against you! (Psalm 18:38) And remember to expose the enemy once you have destroyed him! (Joshua 10:24,25)

CANCEL OUT NEGATIVE INFLUENCE EACH DAY

You have the authority to cancel out negative influences that are coming against you. Daily confession of the Word of GOD and daily prayer is essential in fighting the enemy.

Confess this prayer daily as the Holy Spirit reveals to you the "enemies" that are pressing against you. As he reveals your "enemies", list them on the Personal Inventory List at the back of Chapter 6. Keep a pen and notebook with you at all times to record all that GOD reveals to you. Your prayer list should include what GOD has shown you about yourself. This information will be part of your personal fighting manual. The following prayer is meant to be a guide to show you how warfare prayer can be done and give you examples. You will need to personalize the prayers and include words that are pertinent to you. As you use the manual, you will be more open to hear GOD and what He is saying to you personally.

CONFESS THIS PRAYER EVERYDAY:

"The devil is a liar.
Let every word of GOD be true.
I am qualified to fight and I am dangerous.

I cover myself, my children, my spouse, my home,
my car, my job, my pastors, my church,
my entire bloodline, everything I own
with the Blood of Jesus."

SPEAK !   "I call forth the Spirit of adoption,
whereby I cry, Abba, Father! Help me
Father, I yield myself to your truth,
your word, your will."
"Principalities, spiritual wickedness
in high places, rulers of darkness over
(your area), you are bound from my life,
where I walk, where I work, where I live,
Wherever I am, you are bound,
In Jesus Name."

"I cancel all negative words spoken against
me. I cancel their effect and I send
them back from whence they have come.
I send confusion back into the enemy's camp."

"You are bound when I am asleep and
when I am awake . . . you are bound!
Let go of me. Leave me, in Jesus Name."

"Principalities, spiritual wickedness
in high places, rulers of darkness,
GOD has called me Prosperous. Let go
of my finances. Let me go in Jesus Name.
Let go of my children, my spouse. They
are the blessed and called of GOD and
they are taught of the Lord. Let go of
my emotions for they are hidden in Christ.
You have no right to them. I condemn you.
Jealousy in me and on me — let go because
GOD has granted me favor with men. I speak

peace to all those that rise up and speak
against me. Hold your peace!! In Jesus Name."
"I reject and cancel all lying spirits and
their effect on me. I reject and cancel
all negative words spoken against me.
I reject and cancel hatred, jealousy,
prejudice, unfairness and the spirit of
lack and its effect — for GOD
has given me favor with men.
I am the righteousness of GOD."
"devil, I cancel every plot, against my peace
and joy, every conspiracy against my health
and prosperity, every story, every strategy
against me, my home, my church, my job,
the Kingdom of GOD, in Jesus Name."

I reject and cancel the spirit of shame
over my life. I cancel its effects in
me and on me. I send shame back where
it came from. I am not ashamed of my life,
for it is hidden in GOD through Christ.

I am satisfied and content in all
that He has given me.
Because I love GOD and carry His
anointing, the enemy hates me, but I glorify
GOD and give Him all honor. I commit my soul
and all that I am to GOD and I continue in
well doing because GOD
is faithful to keep His Word.

Because I suffer for righteousness
sake, I am happy, I am not afraid of the terror
of the enemy and neither am I troubled. I sanctify
the LORD GOD in my heart and even though the enemy
has compassed me about, I am ready at all times

to give an answer to everyone that asks me the
reason for my hope and faith in GOD.

I am not ashamed of my testimony in Jesus Christ.
I am not ashamed of the testimony of Jesus
who bled and died and rose again
to give me life more abundantly.

I am a partaker of the afflictions of the Gospel
according to the power of GOD, not the enemy's
power. Jesus saved me and called me to a holy
calling, not according to works, but according
to His own purpose in GOD
and the enemy cannot stop it.

My Savior Jesus Christ has abolished
death and brought life and immortality to light
through the Gospel. I am not ashamed: for I know
in whom I believe, and am persuaded that He is able
to keep that which I have committed to Him—my
soul, my spirit, my life, my finances, my children,
my spouse, against that day.

Therefore, I hold fast the form of sound words
which I have heard in faith and love in Christ Jesus.
For myself and those in my care, I will hold fast the form of
sound words which I have heard in faith and love
in Christ Jesus for myself and for those I am sent to.

I will keep all that has been committed
to me by the Holy Ghost. Wherein I suffer trouble
as an evildoer(I know that I am not evil) even being
in bounds. But the Word of GOD in me is not bound.
Therefore, I endure all things for the elect's sake,
that they may obtain the salvation which is in Christ
Jesus with eternal glory.

It is a faithful saying;
for if we be dead with Him we shall also reign with Him.
We hold fast the form of sound words which I have heard in faith
and love in Christ Jesus with eternal glory.
Though persecutions, afflictions come to me,
I know that GOD will deliver me from them all.
I watch in all things, I endure
afflictions and do the work of an Evangelist.
I fight the good fight of faith and the LORD shall
deliver me from every evil work and will preserve
me unto His heavenly Kingdom.
To whom be glory forever."

SCRIPTURAL REFERENCES FOR

CHAPTER 4

FIGHT TO KILL

Hebrews 6:18,19

That by two immutable things, in which it was impossible for GOD to lie, we might have a strong consolation, who have fled for refuge to lay hold upon the hope set before us: which hope we have as an anchor of the soul, both sure and steadfast, and which enters into that within the veil;

Joshua 10:8

And the LORD said to Joshua, Fear them not: for I have delivered them into thine hand; there shall not a man of them stand before thee.

Joshua 1:8

This book of the law shall not depart out of thy mouth; but thou shall meditate therein day and night, that thou mat observe to do according to all that is written therein: for then thou shall make thy way prosperous, and then thou shall have good success.

I Timothy 4:15

Meditate upon these things; give thyself wholly to them; that thy profiting may appear to all.

Joshua 1:9

Have I not commanded thee? Be strong and of good courage; be not afraid, neither be thou dismayed: for the Lord thy GOD is with thee whithersoever thou goes.

Joshua 10:19, 24-25, 33, 36-39

And stay ye not, but pursue after your enemies, and smite the hindermost of them; suffer them not to enter into their cities: for the LORD your GOD hath delivered them into your hand. (24) And it came to pass, when they brought out those kings unto Joshua, that Joshua called for all the men of Israel, and said unto the captains of the men of war which went with him, Come near, put your feet upon the necks of them. (25) And Joshua said unto them, Fear not, nor be dismayed, be strong and of good courage: for thus shall the Lord do to all your enemies against whom you fight. (33) Then Horam king of Gezer came up to help Lachish; and Joshua smote him and his people, until he had left him none remaining. (36) And Joshua went up from Eglon; and all Israel with him, unto Hebron; and they fought against it; (37) And they took it, and smote it with the edge of the sword, and the king thereof, and all the cities thereof, and all the souls that were therein; he left none remaining, according to all that he had done to Eglon; but destroyed it utterly, and all the souls that were therein.(38) And Joshua returned, and all Israel with him, to Debir; and fought against it: (39) And he took it, and the king thereof, and all the cities thereof; and they smote them with the edge of the sword, and utterly destroyed all the souls that were therein; he left none remaining: as he had done to Hebron, so he did to Debir, and to the king thereof; as he had done also to Libnah, and to her king.

Psalms 18:34, 37-42 (Today's English Version)

(34) He trains me for battle so that I can use the strongest bow. (37) I pursue my enemies and catch them; I do not stop until I destroy them; (38) I strike them down and they cannot rise; they lie defeated before me. (39) You give me strength for the battle and victory over my enemies. (40) You make my enemies run from me. I destroy those who hate me. (41) They cry for help, but no one saves them; they call to the LORD but He does not answer. (42) I crush them, so that they become like dust which the wind blows away. I trample on them like mud in the streets.

Study Questions

Chapter 4

FIGHT TO KILL

1. In what ways can you put away fear?
   _____
   _____
   _____

2. Can you cancel out any negative influences?
   _____
   _____
   _____

3. What does being strong and having good courage mean to you?
   _____
   _____
   _____

4. What scriptures from your reading would be beneficial for you to meditate on?
   _____
   _____
   _____

Chapter 5

SPEAKING THE PROMISES OF GOD

It is written, that man shall
Not live by bread alone,
But by every word that proceeds
Out of the mouth of GOD.
Jesus

After 40 days in the wilderness, Jesus was hungry, and the devil tempted Him to turn stone into bread. Jesus answered him with the Word: (Luke 4:4) When the devil tempted Jesus to worship him instead of GOD, Jesus answered: Get thee behind me, satan; for it is written, "Thou shall worship the Lord thy GOD, and Him only shall thou serve." (Luke 4:8) And when satan tempted Jesus, saying: "cast thyself down from hence: For it is written, He shall give His angels charge over thee, to keep thee." (Luke 4:9-10), Jesus answering said unto him: "It is said, Thou shall not tempt the LORD thy GOD." (Luke 4:12) When the devil had ended all the temptation, he departed from Jesus for a season and Jesus returned to Galilee in the power of the Spirit. He went into the synagogue and identified Himself by reading Isaiah:

"The Spirit of the LORD is upon me, because he hath anointed me to preach the gospel to the poor: He hath sent me to heal the brokenhearted, to preach deliverance to the captives, and recovering of sight to the blind, to set at liberty them that are bruised, to preach the acceptable year of the LORD. (Luke 4:18-19)

Speaking the Word of GOD is a powerful tool that can be used to increase your faith, AND IT IS THE MOST IMPORTANT WEAPON IN YOUR ARMORY against satan.

The Scriptures are full of the promises GOD has made to us. We can remind ourselves of them daily. Jesus spoke the Scriptures to satan and satan left. Jesus spoke the Word of GOD to identify Who He was and what His purpose and destiny were. You must also use the Word of GOD as the ultimate weapon against your enemies. For every "enemy", for every attack that satan sends against you, there are Scriptures to counterattack satan and move him off you and out of your way. There are Scriptures that will build you up and fortify you and give you the identity that GOD meant for you to have in Him.

When you cancel out your negative traits as you become aware of them, there are spaces left in your soul that must be refilled with good, positive traits. You can draw to yourself positive Godly character. **The righteousness of GOD can no longer cover these sins, but must be given the opportunity to replace them.**

In the same way that you are recognizing negative traits and canceling their effect on you, you can speak the promises of GOD into your own life by drawing them to you. Creating your own opportunities for happiness is being in the divine will of GOD. **You can pursue personal liberty and freedom to obtain the blessings of GOD.**

This can be done by drawing certain qualities into your life by speaking the Word of GOD that states the Covenant of the Promised Land. GOD promises in the New Covenant to write His Words upon our hearts. In other words, we will know the Word because it will be in us. **Speaking the Word of GOD or actually verbalizing it helps you to memorize it and it also records it in your spirit and allows the Word of GOD to literally become part of your being.**

Put these positive Godly Scriptures in your mind and heart by speaking them every day.

SPEAK:

"Because GOD's Spirit is upon me,
I am healed and delivered. (Luke 4:18)
GOD loves me, so much that he sent Jesus
so that I would not perish but have
everlasting life. (John 3:16)
Jesus has come and He is alive and
I have abundant life. (John 10:10)
Because I live by Jesus (John 6:57),
I am dead to sin and alive to
righteousness (I Peter 2:24). I am
Jesus' beloved and I live in divine
health and I am prosperous (III John 2).
Jesus has overcome the world (John 16:33)
and has spoken unto me so that I might
have peace. My peace is perfect because
I keep my mind stayed on Him (Isa. 26:3).
Therefore, I rejoice and I rejoice evermore
because my joy is full everyday (John 15:11)
The Joy of the LORD is my strength (Ne. 8:10)
and I am strong in the LORD and in the Power
of His might. (Eph. 6:10)

There is quality of life that GOD has promised in His Word. That life is perpetual and abundant. That life is yours according to the Covenant GOD has established with you. That covenant says, "If I obey GOD, I will eat the fat of the Land and I shall be blessed in all that I put my hand to. (Deut. 28:1-14) . . . that everywhere I place the souls of my feet is mine. (Jos.1:3)

I WILL SPEAK, DO AND DRAW THE THINGS TO ME I LOVE:

I DRAW:

(Place your desires here)

Personal Freedom   ————
Creativity in Thought and Design   ————
Awareness of GOD's Voice   ————
Awareness of GOD's Presence   ————
Serenity and Peace   ————
Ease   ————
Stability   ————
Aliveness   ————

I DRAW TO MYSELF RIGHT NOW: (QUALITIES YOU DESIRE)

Obedience   ————
Diligence   ————
Compassion   ————
Quietness   ————
Boldness   ————
Discernment of the Body   ————
Loyalty   ————
Gentleness   ————
Humility   ————
Faith   ————
Alertness   ————
Joy   ————
Abundance   ————
Wealth   ————
Discerning of Spirits   ————
Wisdom to know what to do after discernment   ————

Peace   _____
Love   _____
Perpetual Prosperity   _____
Favor of GOD and man   _____
More than enough seed   _____
Consistency in obedience to GOD   _____
Contrition   _____
Compassion   _____
Earnestness in prayer   _____
Desire to seek GOD   _____

SPEAK:

I am successful and prosperous and victorious
In every area of my life, As a man/woman,
As a father/mother, on my job,
In every relationship,

Everywhere the sole of my foot treads,
In business, in love, in finances . . .
In life . . . I am successful.

I DRAW THESE QUALITIES TO MYSELF NOW!

Faith
Financial Security
Peace
Abundance
Favor of GOD and Man
Independence
Favor in the Workplace

GOD said He would give you the desires of your heart (Ps. 34.7).
The next list will be all the things that you have a desire for. No matter

what that desire is — no matter how much it costs, begin to speak those desires out and draw then to you. GOD puts desires in you so that He can fulfill them for His glory. So be specific as you take your time to add to your list daily.

I DRAW TO ME THE FOLLOWING THINGS:

WEALTH   _____

BETTER JOB   _____

BETTER CAR   _____

BETTER HOME   _____

EDUCATION   _____

CLOTHING   _____

THEN SPEAK THIS:

"I am called to be successful.
I will not go any other way
Except the way that GOD desires me to go.
No matter what comes, I shall overcome
Because the greater one lives in me.
I heed his voice."

"No one shall cause me to deviate
From the path that GOD has called me to walk.
No one shall cause me to be ashamed,
Because I glory in Christ and obey his voice.
I rejoice in the Lord, my GOD, and I shall
Succeed in Jesus' Name."
"I am successful in all things
That the Lord has given me to do.
I desire to do and complete every assignment

That GOD has given me.
Nothing will stand in my way
Because it is my will to do the will of the father.

Each day, I will seek GOD for direction
And a clear path for His work to be completed in me."

SCRIPTURAL REFERENCES FOR

CHAPTER 5

SPEAKING THE PROMISES OF GOD

LUKE 4:4

It is written, that man shall not live by bread alone, but by every word of GOD.

LUKE 4:8

Get thee behind me, satan; for it is written, "Thou shall worship the Lord thy GOD, and Him only shall thou serve.

LUKE 4:9-10

And when satan tempted Jesus, saying: "cast thyself down from hence: For it is written, He shall give His angels charge over thee, to keep thee.

LUKE 4:12

Jesus answering said unto him: "It is said, Thou shall not tempt the LORD thy GOD.

LUKE 4:18-19

The Spirit of the LORD is upon me, because he hath anointed me to preach the gospel to the poor: He hath sent me to heal the brokenhearted, to preach deliverance to the captives, and recovering of sight to the blind, to set at liberty them that are bruised, to preach the acceptable year of the LORD.

JOHN 3:16

For GOD so loved the world, that He gave His only begotten Son that whosoever believeth on Him should not perish, but have everlasting life.

JOHN 10:10

The thief cometh not, but for to steal, and to kill, and to destroy: I am come that they might have life, and have it more abundantly.

JOHN 6:57

As the Living Father hath sent me, and I live by the Father: so he that eats me shall live by me.

I PETER 2:24

Who his own self bare our sins in his own body on the tree that we being dead to sins, should live unto righteousness: by whose stripes you were healed.

III JOHN 2

Beloved I wish above all things that thou may prosper and be in good health even as your soul prospers.

JOHN 16:33

These things have I spoken unto you, that in Me ye might have peace, In the world ye shall have tribulation: but be of good cheer, I have overcome the world.

ISAIAH 26:3

Thou wilt keep him in perfect peace, whose mind is stayed on Thee: because he trusts in thee.

JOHN 15:11

These things have I spoken unto you, that my joy might remain in you, and that your joy might be full.

PSALMS 34:7

The angel of the LORD encamps round about them that fear Him, and delivers them.

EPHESIANS 6:10

Finally, my brethren, be strong in the LORD, and in the power of His might

DEUT. 28:1-14

And it shall come to pass, if thou shall hearken diligently unto the voice of the LORD thy GOD will set thee on high above all nations of the earth: (2) And all these blessings shall come on thee, and overtake thee, if thou shall hearken unto the voice of the LORD thy GOD. (3) Blessed shall thou be in the city, and blessed shall thou be in the field. (4) Blessed shall be the fruit of thy body, and the fruit of thy ground, and the fruit of thy cattle, the increase of thy kine, and the flocks of thy sheep.

(5) Blessed shall be thy basket and thy store. (6) Blessed shall thou be when thou comes in, and blessed shall thou be when you go out.(7) The LORD shall cause thine enemies that rise up against thee to be smitten before thy face; they shall come out against thee one way, and flee before thee seven ways. (8) The LORD shall command the blessing upon thee in thy storehouses, and in all that thou set thine hand unto; and he shall bless thee in the land that the LORD thy GOD gives thee.

(9) The LORD shall establish thee a holy people unto Himself, as He hath sworn unto thee, if thou shall keep the commandments of the LORD thy GOD, and walk in His ways. (10) And all the people of the earth shall

see that thou art called by the Name of the LORD; and they shall fear thee. (11) And the LORD shall make thee plenteous in goods, in the fruit of thy body, and in the fruit of thy cattle, and in the fruit of thy ground, in the land which the LORD swear unto thy fathers to give thee.

(12) The LORD shall open unto thee His good treasure, the heaven to give the rain unto thy land in its season, and to bless all the work of thine hand: and thou shall lend unto many nations and thou shall not borrow. (13) And the Lord shall make thee the he head and not the tail; and thou shall be above only, and thou shall not be beneath; it thou that hearken unto the LORD thy GOD, which I command thee this day, you observe them and to do them: (14) And thou shall not go aside from any of the words which I command thee this day, to the right hand, or to the left, to go after other gods, to serve them.

JOSHUA 1:3

Every place that the sole of your foot shall tread upon, that have I given unto you.

NOTES

MY PERSONAL DESIRES	QUALITIES I DESIRE	I DRAW THESE QUALITIES

NOTES

Chapter 6

JUDGE YOURSELF
(So GOD Doesn't Have To)

For if we judge ourselves we should not
Be judged, we are chastened of the Lord,
That we should not be condemned with the world.
(1 Corinthians 11:31, 34)

As many as the Lord loves,
He rebukes and chastens.
So be zealous therefore and repent.
(Revelation 3:19)

IT IS TIME NOW TO GET SERIOUS ABOUT ALLOWING
GOD TO SHINE HIS LIGHT ON EVERY SIN, EVERY
HINDRANCE AND EVERY PERSONALITY PROBLEM, AND
EVERY GIANT THAT IS KEEPING US FROM A CLOSER
WALK WITH HIM.

GOD is dealing with a lot of us at arm's length because the stench
of our personal sin won't let him come any closer. I don't want GOD
to deal with me like He is putting a pair of stinking sneakers out of
the house with one hand and holding His Nose with the other. I
want to come face-to-face with GOD. I want to come boldly before
the throne of grace—I want to stand in His presence and see Him
as He is—Holy and blameless. I want to say just as Jesus did, "The

Prince of this world has nothing in me." (John 14:30) I want to be a "sweet smelling savor" in the nostrils of GOD but the truth is most of us who proclaim salvation and profess Jesus as Lord, stink in the nostrils of GOD.

We all love something that smells good. Women and men are up on the latest designer scents and they buy them to smell good for each other. Well, let's learn how to be a designer fragrance for GOD! We all know what a pleasant fragrance can do for us. Just think about what it will do for GOD! Let us offer to GOD as a sweet smelling savor, a zealous search of ourselves and a zealous repentance from that which we had been ignorant of. (Num.15:24-26)

As long as we carry sin there is a part of us that will be unpleasant odor to GOD. But, if we tenaciously judge ourselves and become aware of our own "beams" (Math.7:13) that are in our own eyes, and actively repent, the fragrance of that kind of humility will be very pleasing to GOD. Each of us has our own fragrance that we can offer to GOD. Nobody can use your fragrance. You can't loan it to anyone and nobody can take it and use it. You and only you can send your personal fragrance to GOD as often as you like—as much as you like or as much as needed. You are GOD's perfume so let your fragrance be a humble heart and a contrite spirit and GOD will not despise you. (Psalm 34:18) . . . "GOD dwells in a High and Holy Place, (and) with him also that is of a contrite and a humble spirit, to revive the spirit of the humble, and to revive the spirit of the contrite ones." (Isa.57:15)

HUMBLE AND CONTRITE ARE ACTION VERBS

Humble and contrite are action verbs and you are participating in the action. Humble means to humiliate or abase—to bring down or make low. Contrite means to smite—to break in pieces—to REPENT! Actively humble yourself by judging your own sin before GOD has to!

Break your own heart into pieces and examine them. Chasten yourself in the light of the Word of GOD before GOD has to and **REPENT!** Remember not to be passive about sin and don't passively wait around until someone else or GOD Forbid—JEHOVAH Himself has to judge you. Actively participate in your own freedom by daily judging yourself. GOD will revive you and He will restore you and He will dwell with you.

TAKING INVENTORY

Taking personal inventory of all that we do and say on a daily basis can be a great undertaking. Many of us already pride ourselves on asking GOD to search our hearts—to know our ways and reveal hidden and secret sin. But most of us pray this way not really owning up to the fact that sin is our hearts. Let someone try to talk to you about your shortcomings—you don't receive it! A number of years ago, the LORD tried for over a year to tell me through different people that I had pride. My Pastor told me first and I didn't believe him. My response to him was, "Me . . . Pride!? Surely, you jest!" And I was praying all the time for the LORD to search my heart.

It was a battle and very hard to accept that someone as righteous as I had a sin like pride. After all, I had been saved fifteen years—there's no way that I could have pride! Well, I did and "big time", too!! The recognition of that and the fact that I couldn't receive it at first started me on my journey to seek and search myself in the light of the scriptures. I made up my mind that I would hear from anyone what my shortcomings are because GOD can and will use anyone and anything He wants to talk to His people, after all He did use a donkey. (Num.22:28)

JUDGE YOURSELF

Ask yourself:

Have I wounded anyone today? Have I walked in my own willful way? Father, in Jesus Name, reveal hidden secret sin. As you pray that prayer earnestly and honestly, the LORD will reveal your problems. Write them on your Inventory List and pray against each item each day. An Inventory List is a compilation of all your personality traits that do not give glory to GOD. These are the "giants" discussed in chapter three that you will put on your Personal Menu each day. When you begin to seek GOD earnestly to reveal your secret sin, He will begin to answer you by showing you yourself. Not your neighbor, not your spouse but **GOD will show you *yourself!***

Don't be afraid to listen to what the HOLY SPIRIT will say to you about you. He will say it directly to you, through the Word of GOD, spoken, preached, or written. Most of the time, the only person your sin is hidden from is you. Everyone around you knows you and can see you in ways that are hidden from yourself.

For those who are really serious about finding out what their hidden sins are, ask someone you trust, like your Pastor, a close friend or relative, or your spouse what they see in you that is a negative personality trait—something you can work on getting rid of. This suggestion is not for the purpose of starting World War III, but to get you used to hearing about what's wrong with you. As they begin to tell you, be meek, humble, and patient. Let them finish. This is not a time to have unbelief. Remember that "love believes all things". (I Cor.13:7)

As the LORD speaks to you and others share their insight, your Inventory List will grow. Each day in your personal prayer time, you will cancel out these negative traits and draw to yourself positive traits. At times you will be able to cross traits off your Inventory List because you will know that GOD has completely delivered you from them. But, don't be too hasty to cross them off because certain troublesome spirits have their root in areas we have not understood. Sometimes, because we don't feel that particular oppression anymore, does not mean it is completely gone. It is not gone until the root has been dug up and cast out by the Spirit of GOD. Wait before you stop canceling out troublesome spirits. Wait until you have release by the Spirit of GOD that it is gone. Don't go according to your feelings. On the other hand, there will be negative traits that will leave instantly. Again, trust the release that you will get from the Holy Spirit.

Sometimes, we are not aware of problems that we are having or tendencies to certain sin. Sometimes we will get a nudge or a slight uneasiness in our heart when certain subjects are mentioned. This is a sign to us that we need to explore what that uneasiness is about. Where is it coming from? There is a reason for it. Seek GOD! Ask GOD for clarity and don't let it slide! Remember, we must be more alert than we ever were before. Ask GOD to reveal what the root of that uneasiness is and when He does, receive it! "Don't hide yourself from your own flesh." (Isa. 58:7) Knowledge is the key here and GOD would not have you ignorant to satan's devices. (II Cor.2:11)

ASK FORGIVENESS

Once sins that were hidden to you have been revealed, repent. Ask GOD's forgiveness. Don't condemn yourself when you begin to see what a wretch you really are. Don't become guilty. However, if condemnation and guilt are negative traits that you possess, add them to your Inventory List and cancel out their effects each day until they are completely gone—until you are totally delivered. Now we need wisdom on how to deal with what is breathing against us. Now is the time to be patient and rest in GOD. Don't panic! Answers and deliverance are coming soon enough. Peace . . . rest . . . and wait for all of the wisdom that your search will bring. GOD didn't bring you this far to let you go.

Continue quietly resting in your search and GOD will do it! He may not reveal wisdom to you when you are on your knees waiting for HIM to speak. He may come when you are in the bath or listening to a sermon, or driving down the highway or at anytime. So be prepared. Be ready to listen. Be alert and aware of GOD's voice and remember, you have everything you need to win the battle at your disposal. And the battle is for your very life—the life that was promised you through Jesus Christ—Life that is peaceful, abundant, prosperous and healthy.

The following list contains personality traits, enemies and the giants you can be bothered by each day. Some you will recognize immediately—others you will learn to allow the Holy Spirit to reveal to you—still others do not pertain to you. However, all of them are enemies and enemies to GOD's purpose in you. They are the "giants" in the land that are keeping you from abundant life.

When you recognize which ones you are bothered by, begin to fight them using the confession and prayer in chapter four. There is also a place to record them at the end of chapter four. Fight these enemies one-by-one until they are all defeated. Put them on your menu each day and "eat 'em for lunch".

Fight to kill! Utterly destroy them and leave none remaining!
Remember to be alert to what the Holy Spirit is telling you and act on it immediately whether you can see it or not. Keep strong for the battle by constantly undergirding yourself with The Peace and Joy of Jesus.

FIGHT! FIGHT TO WIN!
And fight with the knowledge that GOD has already caused you to triumph. You have already won! You are victorious, but you cannot be a champion unless you fight!

Ambivalence	Infirmity
Abandonment	Jealousy
Anger	Lying
Addiction	Lust
Arrogance	Lack
Bondage	Lack of Control
Covetousness	Laziness
Confusion	Laziness in Prayer
Control	Loneliness
Double-mindedness	Looking Back
Deception	Misconception
Deceitfulness	Pain
Depression	Panic
Discouragement	Paranoia
Division	Procrastination
Disrespect	Blockage
Doubt	Poverty
Elitism	Pride
False Personality	Resentment

Familiarity
Fear
Fear of Rejection
Feeling Unwanted
Feeling Neglected
Gluttony
Gossip
Greed
Guilt
Haughtiness
Heaviness
Idolatry
Impatience
Inadequacy
Inconsistency
Insecurity
Intellectualism

Rebellion
Rejection
Restlessness
Sadness
Shame
Stealing
Selfishness
Sluggishness
Self hatred
Self pity
Self-centeredness
Unbelief
Unforgiveness
Unholy conversation
Worry

JUDGE YOURSELF

*If a man therefore purge himself from these,
He shall be a vessel unto honor, sanctified
And meet for the master's use, and prepared
Unto every good work. (II tim.2:21)*

COMING CLEAN BEFORE GOD

Each day you will go over your Inventory List during prayer. **Pray this prayer for each of the items on the list that pertain to you and expect GOD to remove them:**

*Have mercy upon me, O GOD according to thy
loving kindness: according unto the
multitude of thy tender mercies, blot
out my transgressions. (Ps. 51:1)*

Wash me thoroughly from mine iniquity
and cleanse me from my sin. (Ps.51:2)
Create in me a clean heart, O GOD,
and renew a right spirit within me. (Ps.51:10)

SURRENDER EVERYTHING TO GOD

Father, in Jesus Name, I surrender right now.
I surrender myself, all that I am, all that I am
supposed to be all my desires, to be
what you want me to be.
I fully commit my
will and my way to you
and I surrender and now
repent of the following sin and I surrender my
desire for them to you.
Thank you, Father for setting me free.
I surrender . . . .

PLACE YOUR ITEMS HERE:

_____   _____

_____   _____

_____   _____

_____   _____

_____   _____

You are not alone.

(Mat.28:20) Jesus is with you, leading you and guiding you through this purification period. (Pro.3:6) Don't allow pride (Ob.3) to stop you from seeing and releasing all sin oppressing you—sin caught up and mixed up in your personality—sin that oppressed you daily that you've become so accustomed to that you think it's the way it hast to be. You don't have to remain the same. You can conquer anger, lust, perversion or any other sin that so easily besets you by laying it aside and allowing Jesus to take them away one by one. (Heb.12:1)

Be ruthless about cleansing yourself daily.

It isn't enough to recognize the sin. You must also confess it and admit you are powerless over it in your own strength. (1John1:9, James 5:16) Once you repent and turn away from it, the strength of Jesus will be at your side to deliver you and set you totally free. You must know that with the strength of Jesus you can do all things—(Phil.4:13) That all things are possible (Mk.9:23, 10:27) and you can say unto the mountain, (any mountain) be thou removed and every mountain will be made low and a way for you. (Isa.49:11)

Don't fool yourself!

Don't hide from your own flesh. (Isa. 58:7) There will be times when you won't have to ask GOD to reveal hidden—secret sin because you are fully aware of the sin that besets you!! In other words, you already know what your problem is so stop playing games with GOD and with yourself! (ISA.58:7) At those times, **repent instantly—on the spot—and without delay!**

SCRIPTURAL REFERENCES FOR

CHAPTER 6

JUDGE YOURSELF

I Corinthians 11:29.31.32

(28) But let a man examine himself, and so let him eat of that bread, and drink of that cup. (31) For if we would judge ourselves, we should not be judged. (32) But when we are judged, we are chastened of the LORD, that we should not be condemned with the world.

Revelation 3:19

As many as I love, I rebuke and chasten, be zealous therefore, and repent.

Proverbs 3:11, 12

(11) My son despise not the chastening of the LORD: neither be weary of His correction; (12) For whom the LORD loves He corrects; even as a father the son in whom He delighted.

Hebrews 12:11

Now no chastening for the present seems to be joyous, but grievous, nevertheless afterward it yields the peaceable fruit of righteousness unto them which are exercised thereby.

John 7:24

Judge not according to the appearance, but judge righteous judgement.

Lamentations 3:40

Let us search and try our ways, and turn again to the Lord.

II Corinthians 13:5

Examine yourselves, whether ye be in the Faith, Prove your own selves. Know ye not your own selves, how that Jesus Christ is in you, except ye be reprobates?

John 14:30

. . . For the prince of this world cometh, and hath nothing in me.

Numbers 15:24-26

Then it shall be, if ought be committed by ignorance without the knowledge of the congregation, that all the congregation shall offer one young bullock for a burnt offering, for a sweet savor unto the LORD, with his meat offering, and his drink offering, according to the manner, and one kid of the goats for the sin offering.

Matthew 7:13

Enter you in at the straight gate: for wide is the gate, and broad is the way that leads unto life, and few be that find it.

Psalm 34:18

The LORD is near unto them that are of a broken heart: and saves such as be of a contrite spirit.

Isaiah 57:15

For thus says the high and lofty One that inhabits eternity, whose name is Holy: I dwell in a high and lofty place and with him also that is of a contrite and humble spirit, to revise the spirit of the humble and to revive the heart of the of the contrite ones.

Numbers 22:28

And the LORD opened the mouth of the ass, and she said unto Balaam, What have I done unto thee that thou smite me these three times.

I Corinthians 13:7

(Love) Beareth all things, believeth all things, hopes all things, endures all things

Isaiah 58:7

Is it not to deal thy bread to the hungry, and that thou bring the poor that are cast out to thy house? when thou see the naked, that thou cover him: and that thou hide not thyself from thine own flesh?

II Corinthians 2:11

Lest satan should get an advantage of us: for we are not ignorant of his devices.

II Timothy 2:21

If a man therefore purge himself from these, he shall be a vessel unto honor, sanctified, and meet for the master's use, and prepared unto every good work.

Psalms 51:1,2,10

(1) Have mercy upon me, O GOD, according to Thy loving-kindness; according unto the multitude of Thy tender mercies blot out my transgressions. (2) Wash me thoroughly from mine iniquity, and cleanse me from my sin, (10) Create in me a clean heart, O GOD; and renew a right spirit within me.

Matthew 28:20

Teaching them to observe all things whatsoever I have commanded you; and lo, I am with you alway even unto the end of the world.

Proverbs 3:6

In all thy ways, acknowledge Him, and He shall direct thy paths,

Obadiah 3

The pride of thy heart hath deceived thee, thou that dwell in the clefts of the rock, whose habitation is high; that says in his heart, Who shall bring me down to the ground.

Hebrews 12:1

Wherefore seeing we are compassed about with so great a cloud of witnesses, let us lay aside every weight, and the sin that so easily besets us, and let us run with patience the race that is set before us.

James 5:16

Confess your faults one to another and pray one for another, that you may be healed for the effectual fervent prayer of a righteous man avails much,

John 5:16

And therefore did the Jews persecute Jesus, and sought to slay Him, because He had done these things on the Sabbath day.

John 1:9

That was a true Light, which lights every man that cometh into the world.

Phil. 4:13

I can do all things through Christ which strengthens me.

Mark 9:23

Jesus said unto him, if thou canst believe, all things are possible to him that believeth.

Mark 10:27

And Jesus looking upon them says. With men it is impossible, but not with GOD: For with GOD all things are possible.

Mark 11:25

And when ye stand praying, forgive, if ye have an ought against any; that your Father which is in Heaven may forgive you your trespasses.

Luke 3:5

Every valley shall be filled, and every mountain and every hill shall be brought low; and the crooked shall be made straight, and the rough ways shall be made smooth;

Isaiah 49:11

And I shall make all MY Mountains a way, and my highways shall be exalted.

Study Questions

Chapter 6

JUDGE YOURSELF

1. Have you ever wounded anyone?

    _____

    _____

    _____

2. Have you ever walked in your own way?

    _____

    _____

    _____

3. What faults do you have?

    _____

    _____

    _____

4. What can you repent of?

    _____

    _____

    _____

5. What are your pressing faults?

    _____

    _____

    _____

6. Have you confessed your faults?

    _____

    _____

    _____

7. Have you started your Inventory?

_____

_____

_____

8. Why or why not?

_____

_____

_____

INVENTORY LIST

Chapter 7

COMMUNING WITH JESUS

Verily, verily, I say unto you, except you
Eat the flesh of the son of man, and
Drink his blood, ye have no life in you.
Whoso eats my flesh, and drinks my
Blood, hath eternal life; and I will
Raise him up at the last day.
For my flesh is meat indeed, and my
Blood is drink indeed. He that eats
My flesh and drinks my blood, dwells
In me, and I in him. As the living father
Hath sent me and I live by the father;
So he that eats me,
Even he shall live by me.
(John 6:53-58)

Jesus said, "If you eat my flesh and drink my blood, you shall live by me." **WE NEED POWER TO LIVE AS GOD WANTS US TO.** As you begin to pray the prayer in Chapter four & five, GOD will begin to reveal more and more negative traits that beset you. Your prayer time will get longer as your Inventory List grows the temptation at this point is to become discouraged and think that you can't possibly get rid of all that stuff. And you're right!!! You can't do it alone, but with Jesus you can.

You are not alone in this purification period.

GOD through the Holy Spirit is leading you to all truth because He wants you healthy, whole and walking in His Divine Light and Power. You have the Holy Trinity—GOD the Father—GOD the Holy Spirit working on your behalf to purge you, cleanse you, restore you, reform you and deliver you.

"Jesus is ever at the right hand of the Father making intercession for you."(Heb.7:25) He said he would never leave you that He would be with you always. (Matt. 28:20) Jesus has all power (Matt.28:18) and He has given that power to us. (Matt.28:18) But before we go into battle, let us look to Jesus because He is the only one who has confronted satan and can make the true statement " . . . **he has nothing in me**."(John 14:30)

Satan had no part in Jesus and our purification is to bring us to the place where we can say the same thing. Jesus has power over satan so why not let Him exercise that power through us and in us. Jesus said: "If you eat my Flesh and drink my Blood, you shall live by Me." (John 6:57) Our puny attempts at life have resulted in guilt, sin and shame. We need forgiveness and restoration. We need reformation and redemption. It is by the Blood of the Lamb that we have been redeemed. Whatever we need deliverance from, it is not our own power to do it. But through the Power of Jesus, "It is not I, but Christ who lives through me." Let us receive from Him all that He has to live this life abundantly. Let us receive all that Jesus has for us to operate in His authority to combat the enemy as He did. Let us be as He is in the earth. As we are called by His Name, let us display in our life the power of that Name—a Name above all Names. Let us walk worthy to be called Christians—to be called Christ-like.

The more you judge yourself, take inventory, ask forgiveness and repent; the closer you will come to GOD.

Your Personal Inventory List may become quite long, but that's fine because before you have communion with the LORD—before you take Jesus' Body and Blood, you must be clean before GOD. It is there in the Communion that the miracle happens. You are gaining His Character, His Strength and His Power. When you have humbled yourself by thanking GOD for all things, taken personal inventory by judging yourself and asking forgiveness for all revealed sin, you are ready to commune with Jesus. Jesus said, "As often as you do this, do it in remembrance of me."(ICor11:25) What you are remembering is the New Covenant GOD established with you through Jesus' death. Jesus said, "Taking His Body and His Blood, you do show His death until He comes again.

Remembering each day what Jesus did and why He did it will cause a continued humility in you because it will constantly serve as a reminder that it is not you or your gifts or your talents or your strength that brought you where you are, but it was the Blood of Jesus, His Power, His life and His Healing Delivering Grace that allows you to continually have victory over every circumstance.

GOD HAS GIVEN THE NEW COVENANT IN THE BLOOD OF JESUS AS A WEAPON AGAINST THE ENEMY

For I have received of the Lord that which also I delivered unto you, that the Lord Jesus, the same night in which he was betrayed, took bread: and when he had given thanks, he brake it, and said, take eat; this is my body, which is broken for you: this do in remembrance of me. After the same manner, also he took the cup, when he had supped, saying, this is the new covenant in my blood: this do you, and oft as ye drink it in remembrance of me. For as often as you eat this bread and drink this cup, ye do show the Lord's death till he come. Wherefore whosoever shall eat of this bread and drink of this cup unworthily. Shall be guilty of the body and the blood of the lord. But let a man examine himself, so let him eat of that bread and drink of that cup. For he that eats and drinks unworthily, eats and drinks damnation to himself, not discerning the Lord's body. For if we would judge ourselves, we would not be judged.

(I Corinthians11:23-32)

Speaking the confessions and praying the prayers of IF YOU FIGHT YOU WILL WIN, the DAILY FIGHTING MANUAL will allow you to regularly examine and judge yourself. You will actively cleanse and purge yourself of your unGOD-like characteristics and then you will be ready to commune with Jesus. Jesus said, "This do you, as often as you drink it in remembrance of me."(I Cor.11:25) Everyday remember Jesus by drinking His

Blood and eating His body. Jesus said, "These words are spirit and they are life."(John 6:63) We need to be quickened by the spirit! (John 6:63) We need all the power we can get to fight the works of satan against us.

Smith Wigglesworth, a great man of GOD, responsible for raising at least 40 people from the dead, including his wife, and other great signs and wonders; did not get out of bed until he had communed with the LORD. He had the elements on his night table already prepared.

Prepare to take on this added power by asking GOD to bless and receive the elements as symbols of the Body and Blood of JESUS. As you are partaking of the Body and Blood of Jesus, speak to Him. He said to remember Him.

Tell JESUS:

> Jesus, I remember your death—that you
> died so that I could have health, peace,
> joy and everlasting life. I remember you,
> JESUS—that you became a curse for me so
> that I would not have to suffer the curse
> of sin and sickness. I remember that You
> did it for me personally. I thank you for
> my freedom. I thank you that you died so that
> I could be delivered from sin and its results.
> Thank you, JESUS.

As you are taking Communion—as you are partaking of the Body and the Blood of Jesus Christ; truly commune with Him.

Speak as you are partaking of the elements:

I live by Jesus. I live by His Life. I live by His Spirit. I live by His Word. I live by His Peace. I live by His Love. I live by His Power. I live by His Glory. I live by His Grace. I live by His Strength. I Live by His Authority. I live by His Humility. I live by His Obedience. I live by His Healing Virtue. I live by His Miracle Working Power. I am He and He is me. I live by what Jesus desires me to do and say because I do what I see Him do and I say what I hear Him say.

Scriptural References for

CHAPTER 7

COMMUNING WITH JESUS

John 6:53-58

Verily, verily, I say unto you, except ye eat the flesh of the son of man, and drink his blood, ye have no life in you. Whoso eats my flesh, and drinks my blood, hath eternal life; and I will raise him up at the last day. For my flesh is meat indeed, and my blood is drink indeed. He that eats my flesh and drinks my blood, dwells in me, and I in him. As the living father hath sent me and I live by the father; so he that eats me, even he shall live by me.

Hebrews 7:25

Wherefore He is able also to save them to uttermost that come unto GOD by Him, seeing He ever lives to make intercession for them.

Matthew 28:20

Teaching them to observe all things whatsoever I commanded you: and lo I am with you alway, even unto the end of the world.

Matthew 28:18

And Jesus came and spoke unto them saying, all power is given unto me in Heaven and in earth.

John 14:30

Hereafter, I will not talk much with you, for the prince of this world cometh and he has nothing in me.

I Corinthians 11:23-32

For I have received of the LORD that which also I delivered unto you, That the LORD Jesus the same night in which He was betrayed took bread: And when he had given thanks, He brake it, and said, take eat; this is MY Body, which is broken for you: this do in remembrance of me. After the same manner also He took the cup, when He had supped, saying, this cup in the new testament in My Blood: this do ye, as often as ye drink it, in remembrance of Me. For as often as ye eat this bread, and drink this cup, ye do show the LORD'S death till He comes. Wherefore whosoever shall eat this bread, and drink this cup of the LORD unworthily, shall be guilty of the body and blood of the LORD. But let a man examine himself, and so let him eat of that bread, and drink of that cup. For he that eats and drinks unworthily, eats and drinks damnation to himself, not discerning the LORD'S body. For this cause many are weak and sickly among you, and many sleep. For if we would judge ourselves we would not be judged. But when we are judged, we are chastened of the LORD, that we should not be condemned with the world.

John 6:63

It is the Spirit that quickens, the flesh profits nothing: the words that I speak unto you, they are spirit and they are life.

Chapter 8

CALLING FORTH THE GIFTS OF GOD IN YOU

Now there are diversities of gifts, but the same spirit.
And there are diversities of operations,
but it is the same GOD which works all in all.
But the manifestations of the Spirit is given
to every man to profit withal.
For to one is given by the Spirit the word of wisdom;
to another the word of knowledge by the same spirit;
To another faith by the same Spirit;
to another the gifts of healing by the same Spirit;
To another the working of miracles;
to another prophecy; to another discerning of spirits;
to another the interpretation of tongues:
But all these works that one and the selfsame Spirit,
dividing to every man severally as He will.
I CORINTHIANS 12:4-11

Now that you have canceled out negative spirits, you have drawn GOD's positive traits to you, you have given thanks, judged yourself, asked forgiveness and you have communed with the LORD, you are squeaky clean for the day. You can now CALL FORTH THE GIFTS OF GOD IN YOU. GOD has given gifts unto men for the edification of the Body (Eph. 4:11-13) of Christ. The Bible says; "Covet earnestly the best gifts." (I Cor. 12:31)

Boldly stir up the gifts inside of you.

Having the Gifts of GOD operable in and through you is a definite plus to the Body of Christ and a weapon against the enemy. So boldly stir up the gifts, callings and talents in you. When you boldly call on your gifts, they will come.

Speak:

"Gifts of GOD that are within me, come forth;
stir up within me, come forth in Jesus Name".

Don't do this one time and wait, but continue to call forth the gifts of GOD in you until they manifest.

Say:

I stir up the Gifts of GOD that have
been given to me by the Spirit of GOD.
Gifts of GOD, you belong to me, and I
will not allow afflictions to stop me
from using all the gifts that GOD has
given me and I will not be afraid
because GOD has not given me a spirit
of fear, but Love, Power, a sound mind
and nine gifts of the Spirit.
Gifts, you will not leave this
vessel because you are mine,
GOD, the Creator of Heaven and
earth, has given you unto me for
the work of the Kingdom. And this day,

I call you forth up out of me.
Let the Word of the Lord come forth—
let the gifts of GOD come forth.
I call forth the following gifts:
Faith
Wisdom
Working of Miracles
Discerning of Spirits
Creative Miracles
Raising the dead
Miracles like never before that display GOD's Glory
Shekinah Glory of GOD
Gift of Giving
Administration
Mercy
Love

As you are strengthened, the gifts of GOD has given you will pour forth out of you like rivers of living waters.

Only a few gifts are mentioned above. There are many more diverse gifts for the Body of Christ. These you will need to help bring the Body of Christ up to its right place in GOD. The gifts from GOD will also help you fight your enemies. When your enemies are moved out of the way, you can't help but come closer to GOD.

SCRIPTURAL REFERENCES

CHAPTER 8

CALLING FORTH THE GIFTS OF GOD IN YOU

Ephesians 4:11-13

And He gave some apostles, some prophets, some evangelists, pastors and teachers: For the perfecting of the saints, for the edifying of the body of Christ: Till we all come in the unity of the faith. and of the knowledge of the Son of GOD, unto a perfect man, unto the measure of the stature of the fullness of Christ.

I Corinthians 12:31

But covet earnestly the best gifts: and yet show I unto you a more excellent way.

I Corinthians 12:4-11

Now there are diversities of gifts, but the same spirit. And there are diversities of operations, but it is the same GOD which works all in all. But the manifestations of the Spirit is given to every man to profit withal. For to one is given by the Spirit the word of wisdom; to another the word of knowledge by the same spirit; To another faith by the same Spirit; to another the gifts of healing by the same Spirit; To another the working of miracles; to another prophecy; to another discerning of spirits; to another the interpretation of tongues: But all these works that one and the selfsame Spirit, dividing to every man severally as He will.

Chapter 9

TESTIMONY OF JESUS CHRIST

"Declare his glory
among the heathen;
His marvelous works
among the nations."
(1 Chronicles 16:24)

THE TESTIMONY OF JESUS CHRIST IS ONE OF THE MOST POWERFUL WEAPONS OF WARFARE AGAINST THE FORCES OF DARKNESS.

Each day as you pray and fight, satan, you will see the miraculous in your life. As you use all of the weapons GOD has given you, you will begin to win battle after battle. You will begin to walk in victory after victory. You will have testimonies of GOD's GLORY in your life. GOD tells us in His Word to "declare His Glory among the heathen; His marvelous works among the nations." As we give thanks to GOD, call upon His Name and make known His deeds among the people, we can sing a new song of praise to Him each day as we talk of His wondrous works.

The Testimony of Jesus Christ one of the most powerful weapons of warfare against the forces of darkness. There is an anointing—a special grace that GOD sends within the testimony. GOD inhabits the praises of His people. He is present in a special way when you praise Him, thank Him and GLORIFY Him. In GOD's presence is everything that He is. PEACE—JOY—HEALING—DELIVERANCE—LOVE and this anointing destroys every yoke.

EXPOSE GOD'S ENEMIES BY TESTIFYING TO JESUS IN YOUR LIFE.

While you are showing forth GOD'S GLORY, you are also uncovering the tactics of the enemy.

You are exposing the enemy's deeds. We must make an open show of our enemies as part of our warfare. Colossians 2:15 says that Jesus, spoiled principalities and powers and made a show of them openly, triumphing over them. It was for this purpose that the Son of GOD was manifested, to destroy the works of the evil one.

Jesus is the Victor and He has made us victorious through faith in Him.

Joshua called all of his people and officers together when he had defeated the five kings who warred against him. As a sign of total victory, Joshua instructed them to put their foot upon the necks of the five kings after he had defeated them. With each victory, GOD has given you the neck of your enemies and declaring it will help you to sustain your victory.

Declaring victory will encourage the Body of Christ in their Most Holy Faith. How will the heathen know who Jesus is unless we tell them? How can we exhort each other without letting each other know what he has done for us. Declare Jesus to all the earth—Declare His mighty and wondrous works. Tell the world that He is GOD and that He does marvelous things for those who trust Him. It will not do the world or the body of Christ any good if you hold on to your miracles—if you hold on to your victories. BROADCAST THEM!! TELL IT!! TELL WHAT GOD IS DOING!! When you remember Him each day—when you remember where He has brought you from—how He has healed you—how He has forgiven you—how He has blessed you and blessed you—TELL IT!

Testifying to the Truth of the Covenant

Remember to worship GOD and not yourself as you tell what GOD has done for you. The point is to encourage people and let them know that GOD is working for you. Do not make people jealous and envious by the way you relate your testimony. The work that GOD will do through Jesus in your life, as you stand to tell it—as you stand to testify to the truth of the Covenant that GOD established with us through believing Jesus—tell it with respect and awe for GOD's Mercy. Tell your testimony with confidence. Tell it boldly and remember GOD's compassion on you. **Remember that it is GOD' s work**. Don't boast about yourself, and what you did, but focus on GOD and His work in you.

The Covenant promises of GOD are:

PEACE
LOVE EVERLASTING LIFE
JOY
DIVINE HEALTH
DELIVERANCE
LIBERTY
PROSPERITY
SALVATION FOR OUR FAMILIES

Every instance of GOD bringing these promises into your life should be broadcasted in your family, friends and brothers and sisters in the LORD and to the world. Tell GOD's awesome power on your job and in the streets. Tell of Him while you're shopping and write it in the library. Broadcast it on the internet and tell all who will listen. GOD has done great things and it is marvelous in our eyes! It is wonderful to us! Praise Him for it! The book of Revelations tells us to:

"Worship GOD: for the testimony of Jesus is the spirit of prophecy."(Rev.19:10) Tell everything that GOD has done for you. As you speak of GOD's MERCY to you and His graciousness—the spirit of prophecy will be in operation. The Spirit of Prophecy will powerfully enable your words to be set in the spirit realm. Whoever hears your words will glorify GOD and will be prophesied to that, if GOD can do it for you, He can do it for them, also.

TESTIMONY IS TO BE GIVEN UNCEASINGLY

I have set watchmen upon thy walls, O Jerusalem, which shall never hold their peace day nor night: Ye that make mention of the LORD, keep not silence. (Isa.62:6)*

TESTIMONY IS TO BE GIVEN IN YOUR HOME

. . . he that had been possessed with a devil prayed him that he might be with Him. Howbeit, JESUS suffered him not, but says to him, Go home to thy friends, and tell them how great things the LORD hath done for thee, and hath had compassion on thee. *

TESTIMONY RELATES TO PERSONAL EXPERIENCE

Come and hear all ye that fear GOD, and I will declare what He hath done for my soul. (PSALM 66:6)

TESTIMONY RECOUNTS GOD'S BLESSING

I will mention the loving kindness of the LORD, according to all that the LORD has bestowed upon us, and the great goodness toward the house of Israel, which he hath bestowed on them according to the multitude of his loving kindness. (ISA. 63:7)*

TESTIMONY BURSTS FORTH FROM AN INWARD FIRE

Then I said, I will not make mention of Him, nor speak any more in His Name. But His Word was in mine heart as a burning fire, shut up in my bones, and I was weary with forbearing, and I could not stay. (Jer. 20:9)*

TESTIMONY BECOMES IRREPRESSIBLE

(ACTS 4:20)

For we cannot but speak the things we have seen and heard.*

TESTIMONY IS AN OUTGROWTH OF FAITH

We having the same spirit of faith, according as it is written, I believed, and therefore have I spoken; we also believe, and therefore speak; (II COR. 4:13)*

*   Thomas Chain Reference Bible

SCRIPTURAL REFERENCES FOR

CHAPTER 9

THE TESTIMONY OF JESUS CHRIST

Psalm 22:3

GOD inhabits the praises of His people

Colossians 2:15

Jesus, spoiled principalities and powers and made a show of them openly, triumphing over them.

Revelations 19:10

"Worship GOD: for the testimony of Jesus is the spirit of prophecy."

Isaiah 62:6

I have set watchmen upon thy walls, O Jerusalem, which shall never hold their peace day nor night: Ye that make mention of the LORD, keep not silence.

Psalms 66:6

Come and hear all ye that fear GOD, and I will declare what He hath done for my soul.

Isaiah 63:7

I will mention the loving kindness of the LORD, according to all that the LORD has bestowed upon us, and the great goodness toward the house of Israel, which he hath bestowed on them according to the multitude of his loving kindness.

Acts 4:20

For we cannot but speak the things we have seen and heard.

Jeremiah 20:9

Then I said, I will not make mention of Him, nor speak any more in His Name. But His Word was in mine heart as a burning fire, shut up in my bones, and I was weary with forbearing, and I could not stay.

2 Corinthians 4:13

We having the same spirit of faith, according as it is written, I believed, and therefore have I spoken; we also believe, and therefore speak;

Mark 5:18, 19

. . . he that had been possessed with a devil prayed him that he might be with Him. Howbeit, JESUS suffered him not, but says to him, Go home to thy friends, and tell them how great things the LORD hath done for thee, and hath had compassion on thee.

EPILOG

You have come a long way since beginning this manual. If you have come this far and done all the prayers and exercises, then you are well on your way to becoming the reformed and restored Christian who can begin to see Jesus' reflection in themselves.

You are on a journey that will expand your sensitivities to the ways of GOD and will allow you to walk in boldness and confidence victory after victory—triumph over triumph. You will discern the Body more effectively and significantly deepen your growth in GOD through humility. You will experience a new power in Jesus as you begin to see yourself as an extension of GOD's power on the earth. More than ever you will know that Christ lives in you and you live in Him. Watch your confidence and faith increase as you allow Jesus to express Himself more and more through you.

Spiritual warfare means to fight! If you fight for yourself you will win! GOD has given you weapons that we have talked about in this manual and if you use them, you will win.

So Fight! Smite! Slay!

Destroy all of your enemies and leave none remaining. Put a "giant" on your plate and "eat" one for lunch each day by praying against them. And remember that you are qualified to fight because GOD has given you the equipment to fight with.

Every good soldier knows his weaponry and practices his skills until he is proficient in their use. The weapons of warfare discussed in this manual are:

prayer and meditation
canceling the enemy's power in your life
taking on a fighting attitude
confession
drawing positive qualities
giving thanks
judging yourself
taking inventory
forgiveness
coming clean
communion
calling forth your gifts
testimony

The Ultimate Weapon

All of these weapons are based on the Word of GOD—THE ULTIMATE WEAPON IN SPIRITUAL WARFARE and that which all the other weapons are predicated upon.

This FIGHTING MANUAL is designed for you to equip yourself first with the basic weapons of the army of GOD. A spiritual army that knows that the weapons of their warfare are mighty through GOD in pulling down strongholds. For we wrestle not against flesh and blood, but powers and principalities, against the rulers of darkness and spiritual wickedness in high places. (Ephesians 6:12) And the weapons GOD has given us are sufficient to get the job done.

Be encouraged because you will see your personal enemies fall one-by-one. You will see negative personality traits leave and you will experience a new freedom in Jesus Christ as you develop new positive personally traits. GOD BLESS YOU in your battle and GOD sustain all your victories FOR HIS GLORY.

Everyday remember Jesus by drinking His Blood and eating His body. Jesus said, "These words are spirit and they are life."(John 6:63) We need to be quickened by the spirit! (John 6:63) We need all the power we can get to fight the works of satan against us. Remember Smith Wigglesworth, a great man of GOD, responsible for raising over 40 people from the dead, including his wife; did not get out of bed until he communed with the LORD. He kept the elements on his night table already prepared. You can be prepared too—to fight for yourself and everyone else GOD calls you to intercede for. Fight with all the weapons and tools GOD has given us. Put to use every word of GOD where GOD promises to heal, deliver and set free. And FIGHT TO WIN!!